# Peter and Pamela Grow Up

*by*
## H. W. TAME
**(Diagrams by Noel Watson)**

## PHILLIMORE

*First Published 1960*
*by Darwen Finlayson Limited*

*Reprinted 1963, 1966, 1967, 1969, 1970,*
*1974, 1975, 1977, 1979, 1981, 1984*
*PHILLIMORE & CO. LTD.*
*Shopwyke Hall, Chichester, Sussex*

Printed and bound in Great Britain
by Billing and Sons Limited
Guildford, London, Oxford, Worcester

# Contents

# Diagrams

# Introduction: For Teachers and Parents

Some of you may be surprised to find a book on sex instruction which has been specifically written for the child of eleven, but I am convinced that this is the right age at which some simple, but clear and concise, instruction should be given. There are several factors which have led me to this conclusion.

Firstly, it is important that the growing child should be prepared in advance for the physical changes which he or she may expect during the years of puberty. This is of vital importance in the case of girls, because if menstruation begins without any previous warning, a girl will at best be acutely embarrassed, and at worst extremely frightened and assume that she is seriously ill. I believe it to be the practice of many intelligent parents to forewarn their daughters, but I am afraid that all too frequently the information is not given until menstruation has actually begun, and then often in a very sketchy form.

Secondly, it is important that the child should receive information about the facts of life before his emotional reaction to sex has been awakened. The instruction can only be objective if given before the age of puberty; at that level the child will accept the knowledge quite naturally in the same way as he accepts other knowledge imparted at school.

Thirdly, if a child is not given some form of sex instruction before he leaves his primary school, there is the very real danger that he will learn about sex from older children, when he mixes with them at his Secondary School. Then the information is likely to be acquired furtively and incorrectly and he will therefore be conditioned to the wrong attitude towards sex right from the start.

I think you will agree that these are good reasons why sex instruction should be given during the last year in the Primary School, and in any case not delayed beyond the first year at the Secondary School.

We come now to the consideration of who is the best person to impart this knowledge to the growing child. Some parents may well feel that they and they alone should shoulder the responsibility, and if the right relationship exists between them and their children, and if they are capable of giving the information without embarrassment either to themselves or the child, I am sure that they are right. Many parents do answer their children's questions about sex, as and when they arise, as simply and as naturally as possible. A child of five or six will often ask, 'Where do babies come from?' This can be answered quite simply by telling the child that they grow inside the mother until they are old enough to be born.

Parents may well wait in vain for the next question as to how the baby started to grow in the mother's body. The question may not occur to the child until he is too self-conscious to ask. In that case the subject has to be raised in some other way, if the child is to benefit from having the information at the most appropriate time.

It is this introduction of the subject without a preliminary question which often prevents parents from carrying out their intentions of imparting the knowledge themselves.

The method of presentation used in this book has been tested over a number of years. It follows the course of instruction I give in my Primary School. The idea for the course grew out of a Parent Teacher meeting where it appeared that parents were concerned about this matter and that there was a general wish that children should receive such instruction at school.

I decided to experiment with a course of about six lessons for children in their last year at the Primary School, and I circularized the parents telling them what I proposed to do, offering alternative lessons for the children of those parents who preferred to give the instruction themselves. I expected quite a high proportion of parents to take advantage of this offer, but no one did.

It may be of interest to teachers generally, and to Heads in particular, that during the five years I have been giving these lessons only two children have been withdrawn, and they were both from the same family. Thus I feel I have satisfied an obvious need both of the parents and the children.

I believe that comparatively few Primary Schools give sex instruction as such, and I hope that other teachers may be encouraged by my experience, convinced by the arguments I have advanced, and perhaps helped by this book to introduce similar courses in their schools.

If used in schools, the information in this book can form the basis of a series of six to eight lessons, and I would suggest that the best way is to give the lessons orally, using the diagrams in the book to illustrate the points as they arise. Later, the children should revise and consolidate the lessons by reading the text themselves. May I suggest, also, that it is a good plan not to segregate the girls and boys for these lessons, as this keeps the subject in a right and healthy perspective from the start, and discourages the children from thinking that it is a subject, unlike all other subjects on the school timetable, which can only be discussed with one sex at a time.

The course should end with an 'Any Questions' session. I have found in practice that some children feel too self-conscious to ask an intimate question orally. It is a good plan therefore to tell the children beforehand that the last session will be devoted to questions and these may be submitted in writing. This not only saves the child embarrassment but gives the teacher the opportunity of ensuring that he knows the answers.

I have found that the children manifest a growing interest throughout the course, and their searching questions indicate their obvious eagerness for knowledge on this subject.

Parents who wish to instruct their children themselves, either because they feel that they are the right people to do so, or because sex instruction does not form part of the curriculum of the school their children attend, should find the book equally helpful. If they feel too embarrassed to impart the information themselves, the book can be given to the eleven year old to read, for it was written especially for him. In this case it is better, if possible, to discuss it with him afterwards, to ensure that he has understood what he has read.

As a Marriage Guidance Counsellor, I feel convinced that if we as teachers or parents can engender in our children a healthy and balanced attitude to sex from an early age, many of the difficulties which cause marriages to break up could be avoided.

## ACKNOWLEDGEMENT

I should like to express my grateful thanks to those who have made this book possible. First to Lord Darwen for encouraging me to write it, and for the help and advice he has given me; and secondly to Mr. A. Ingleby, the Education Secretary of the National Marriage Guidance Council, who first aroused my interest in this subject, and who has been kind enough to read the manuscript.

H. W. TAME.

# CHAPTER ONE

# *How Life Begins*

The story of how life begins and how we ourselves develop is both fascinating and exciting. In this book you will read about the changes which you may expect to take place in your own body as you slowly develop from a boy or girl into a young man or woman. Peter and Pamela were a boy and a girl very much like you, and you will soon find that many of the things which happened to them while they were growing up are happening to you. Some of the facts that you will read about in this book are not known by all grown-ups, and in any case I hope parents and teachers will read it too so that you will be able to talk these things over with them.

Have you ever asked yourself what is the difference between something that is alive and something that is not alive? Perhaps you will say, 'That's easy. Things which are not alive cannot move.' But if you pause for a moment you will be able to think of a number of things which are certainly not alive but which can move. A train, a motor car and an aeroplane are three obvious examples. They are certainly not alive but they can move very fast. On the other hand a tree, which we know is alive, because we can see it growing, is always fixed to one spot. So the difference between living and non-living things is not one of movement.

Let us consider growing as a sign of life. Certainly all living things grow. But there are some non-living things which can grow. Perhaps you have been to Cheddar caves and seen those huge stalactites and stalagmites. It is difficult to remember which grows up and which grows down, but both certainly grow, even though very slowly, over thousands of years, and yet they are not alive. So the fact that living things all grow is not a complete answer to my question about the difference between living and non-living things.

The best answer is that all living things reproduce themselves in some way. That means that they can hand on life and produce new plants or new animals and insects. Things which are not alive cannot do this. No one, even in this wonderful age of scientific discovery, has yet found out how to create life.

Life is handed on by a seed in the case of plant life or by an egg in the case of an animal. Some of you have probably planted seeds at one time or another and marvelled that such tiny things could produce huge hollyhocks, big round cabbages and fat juicy turnips. But the story of how animal life is handed on is the most wonderful story of all. When you have finished reading this book, you will know a great deal about how various animals are born; and also how it was that you came to be born yourself, and how one day you may become a father or mother.

All animals hand on life by means of an egg. Perhaps this idea seems strange and fantastic to you, but remember that there are all sorts of eggs apart from birds' eggs.

Think first of what a hen's egg is like. You know that it has a hard shell outside. You will have watched your mother crack the shell and empty the inside of the egg into a frying pan. There are two very distinct parts in it: the yolk and the white. There is, however, another part which you may not have noticed, because you will have to look very closely at the egg, after it has been broken, in order to see it. It is a tiny whitish patch which can be found lying on top of the yolk. This is the part which might one day have grown into a baby chick—if the egg had not been broken. The rest of the egg—the yolk and the white—is really the food for the growing chick.

You may have been lucky enough to see a baby chick coming out of its shell, but if not you can easily find a picture of this happening. You will see that the chick has grown enormously from that tiny whitish blob. By the time it is ready to come out it fills the whole of the inside of the shell, and all the yolk and white have disappeared.

The hard outside shell is there to protect the baby chick whilst it is very tiny, and because no food can be fed to the growing chick through this hard shell, all the food which the chick needs is inside the egg when it is laid. All birds' eggs are like this, but they vary in size. The size of the egg depends on the kind of bird. Large birds like ostriches and swans have big eggs, because their babies are quite large when they are hatched and have needed more food from the egg than smaller birds.

Insects lay eggs too, but of a rather different kind. They are far too small to contain enough food for the baby to grow into an insect of the same shape or anything like the same size as its parents. The white butterfly, which is often to be seen flying around in gardens, is a good example. It is very common, so its development can easily be watched either out of doors in the vegetable patch or indoors in a jam jar. This butterfly is called the cabbage white because it lays its eggs on cabbages. The next time you see one in your garden, look under the cabbage leaves and you may find a cluster of the tiny greenish eggs which it has laid.

One day, quite soon, the eggs will hatch out, not into butterflies—they are too small for that —but into tiny caterpillars. These caterpillars are the next stage in the growth of the butterfly, and they have only one job to do: to eat and eat, and grow big and fat. They have enormous appetites and will very soon eat holes in the leaves of the cabbage.

When they have grown big and fat enough to contain all the food which will be needed for the butterfly to be born, their outside skin grows hard and they turn into a chrysalis. In this

Group of eggs under
a cabbage leaf

Caterpillar whose job
is to eat and eat

Chrysalis in which the
Butterfly is hatched

Butterfly which lays
more eggs

*Diagram* 1
How the Cabbage White Butterfly hands on life.

stage they are something like the hen's egg, because the baby is protected by the hard shell while it is changing and growing. Inside the chrysalis, the fat little caterpillar, which could only crawl slowly across the leaf and gorge itself, is changing into a butterfly. When the change is completed the case splits open and out crawls a butterfly. It rests for a short time, spreads its wings and then flies away to continue the life cycle by laying more eggs.

Another sort of egg which you have probably often eaten is the roe from inside fishes. The herring, which is one of the commonest fish caught round our coasts, is excellent food and when we cut it open we find that it may have a hard or soft roe. Soft roes are found in the male herring and hard roes in the female. The hard roes are really hundreds and thousands of fishes' eggs, which the female herring has not had the chance to lay. Very few of these eggs will become fully grown fish. At all stages of their development, small fish are eaten as food by bigger ones. For this reason the herring needs to lay a great many eggs in order that some may survive. In the case of birds the hard shell protects the egg to some extent, and so ensures that there will be a new generation of chicks. You will see that each species protects itself in one way or another against the extinction of its young. Considering all the hazards which are run by most growing animals, it is wonderful that they not only survive, but flourish as they do.

There is another and much better way of protecting the growing young, and that is for them to grow inside their mothers' bodies during the first stages of their lives. Most animals, including human beings, develop in this way. You yourself grew from an egg into a human baby inside your mother's body. I expect you have seen a very young baby and will know that it is quite big—about twenty inches long. You may also have seen young kittens or puppies soon after they were born. These are smaller than a human baby but larger than many baby animals. The kangaroos which you can see bounding about at the zoo have babies that are only about an inch long. They do not have to face the dangers of the great world outside their mothers' bodies while they are so tiny, because there is a safe refuge for them. In the front of the kangaroo's body is a pouch. The tiny baby kangaroo climbs into this pouch and in there it feeds from its mother and is protected from all harm. As it grows stronger it is able to peer over the top, and climb out, and gradually learn to look after itself.

Every animal begins life as an egg, and you probably think that the bigger the animal the bigger the egg must be. This is not so. The egg from which you grew was very tiny indeed—no bigger than a dot made with a sharp pencil. This may seem impossible, but I can assure you that it is true.

The egg from which you grew was made inside your mother's body in a place called an ovary. This word really means 'a place where eggs are produced', and the hard roes of the female fish are her ovaries. In a herring you will find two roes or ovaries, and all girls and women also have two ovaries. These are inside the lower part of the abdomen and they are about the size of large nuts. During childhood the ovaries grow and develop, but they do not start their work of releasing the eggs until girls reach the age of about eleven or twelve.

At about that age the eggs begin to move

away from the ovaries, at the rate of one a month. Each ovary releases in turn an egg, which is smaller than the dot on an 'i', and the ovaries will go on producing eggs every month until a woman is about forty-five years of age. During that period hundreds of eggs will be released—one every month.

The tiny egg is released very close to the open end of a narrow tube, called the Fallopian tube, which is lined with minute hairs. They move the egg along the passage until it reaches its nesting place, called the uterus, or womb, where it will grow and develop into a proper baby. The womb is like a pear in shape and size, and it is hollow, but its walls are very elastic and muscular. At the lower end of the womb there is another opening also leading into a passage. This one is called the vagina and connects the womb to the outside of the body. The outside opening which is protected by folds of skin is between the legs.

If an egg cell has been fertilized as it moves down the Fallopian tube (I will tell you how this comes about in a later chapter), it soon divides itself into two cells, and these divide into four, and then again into eight and so on.

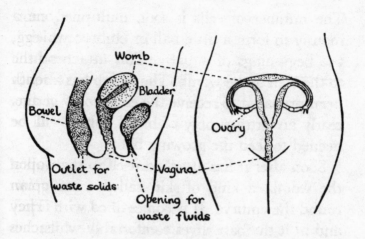

Side view of female sex organs     Front view

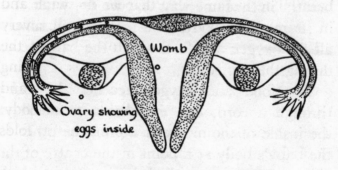

Diagram showing eggs being released from ovary
and their journey to the womb.

*Diagram 2*

The number of cells is soon multiplied enormously to form a little ball or embryo which is the beginnings of a baby. This attaches itself to the wall of the womb. The womb has already been prepared to receive the embryo by getting ready an extra supply of blood, which will be needed to feed the growing baby.

Soon after it has attached itself to the wall of the womb, a kind of skin called a sac grows round the embryo. It becomes filled with liquid and in it the baby lives comfortably whilst it is growing and developing. An unborn baby can live in liquid because it does not have to eat or breathe in the same way that we do, while it is in its mother's body. The mother will supply all the oxygen and food which the baby needs during this period.

The food and oxygen reaches the baby through a cord, one end being attached to the inside of the mother's womb, the other to the baby's body at a point in the centre of the abdomen, correctly called the navel, but which you probably know as the belly button. The cord contains a number of pipes along which flows the mother's blood. The blood carries the food and oxygen which the baby will need if he is to grow. Where the cord is joined to the womb, there is a mass of blood vessels, called the placenta. Some of the blood vessels belong to the baby and some to the mother. It is here that food and oxygen filter through from the mother's blood vessels to those of the baby, and similarly the waste products which collect in the baby's blood are filtered back again into the mother's blood and then disposed of.

The baby continues to grow and develop in its watery sac, tucked away and protected from all harm, inside the mother's womb. The growth is very slow at first and after the egg has been developing for two months the baby is only about an inch long, but the main parts of the body are beginning to appear. After four months the baby has grown much more and is now about five inches long, and by the time the baby is ready to make his appearance in the outside world he has grown to about twenty inches and usually weighs about seven pounds.

The human baby grows for about nine months inside the mother's body, but other animals take varying times to grow from the egg into the animal which is ready to be born. A cat and a dog take about nine weeks to produce their babies, a sheep about five months, a cow about the same time as a human being—nine months, a horse almost a year and the elephant, which of course is the biggest of all the animals, takes nearly eighteen months.

Now let us return to our growing baby and see just how he makes his way from the womb to the outside world. He has been growing there for nine months and during that time he has increased in size enormously. The walls of the womb are very elastic in order to make room for the fully developed infant. When the baby is ready, the walls of the womb stop stretching and begin to squeeze instead. These squeezes, which are sometimes called labour pains, are something like tummy ache to the mother and they give her warning that the baby is nearly ready to be born.

At first the womb only squeezes at intervals of about an hour or so, and this gives the mother time to go to the nursing home, if arrangements have been made for the baby to be born there, or to summon the doctor or the nurse to help her in bringing the baby into the world, if he is to be born at home.

Gradually the intervals between the squeezes get less and less, which means that the birth of the baby is getting near. The baby has been lying inside the womb, usually with his head downwards, and the head is the first part which pushes its way into the vagina. The vagina, like the womb, is very elastic. Although normally it is quite small and much too narrow to permit a baby to pass through, when the womb contracts, the muscles in the vagina expand and make room for the baby to enter it.

By this time the sac of liquid, in which the baby has been growing so comfortably, has burst so that the baby can make his way into the world down the vagina and out through the opening between his mother's legs. He is still attached, by means of the cord I have mentioned, to the placenta which remains, for the time being, inside the mother's body. This cord the doctor or nurse ties and cuts a short distance from the baby's body. Cutting the cord does not hurt the mother or the baby, as there are no nerves in it (just as cutting your finger nails does not hurt). The small piece of cord which is still attached to the baby will very soon dry up leaving the knot in the centre of his abdomen. This is the belly button.

Soon after he is born the baby will give his first cry. This shows that he has started to breathe for himself. Remember that in the nine months that he was growing in his mother's body he had no need to use his lungs. If the baby does not start to breathe immediately he is born, as sometimes happens, the doctor will give him a little tap, and the first cry announces to the world that another human being has been born. The baby then has his eyes and mouth cleaned very gently and is wrapped up warmly to protect him from the colder world outside his mother's womb.

After the baby has been born, the cord, the placenta and the empty bag in which the baby grew have served their purpose and soon the placenta peels away from the wall of the womb and these parts, which are no longer wanted, pass down the vagina and out of the body. They are known as the afterbirth, and when this comes away the birth of the baby has really been completed.

Of course the mother feels tired from the muscular effort involved in bringing the baby

Baby about to be born, head first.

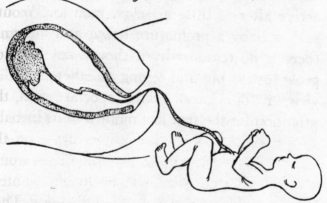

The baby has been born, the cord has still
to be cut and the afterbirth to come away.

*Diagram* 3

into the world, but she soon forgets the pains she felt, in the joy of holding her infant son or daughter in her arms.

During the next few weeks the womb and the vagina shrink back to their normal size, and after the mother has rested for a few days in bed, she is usually fit and strong enough to continue her normal life and care for her baby as well.

It does sometimes happen that a baby is born too soon, and it is not uncommon for it to arrive after as little as seven months. We call such a baby a premature baby, and although there is no reason why it should not live and grow just as big and strong as other boys and girls, it does need extra special care and attention for the first few months of its life.

# CHAPTER TWO

# *The Babies Begin to Grow*

Peter and Pamela were born within a few days of each other. They lived in houses almost opposite in a quiet street of a small country town. The two babies were often taken out in their prams together by their proud mothers, but to start with neither Peter nor Pamela took a great deal of notice of the world around them. Most of the time they were asleep, and when they were awake they were either gurgling happily, or yelling vigorously except when they were being fed. Neither of them could eat the kind of things which you can eat—for one thing, they had no teeth. They were fed on milk every few hours.

The milk which you now drink every day comes from cows, but cows do not really provide milk for your benefit, nor do they produce it to enable the dairy farmer to make a living by selling it. Whenever a cow has a calf, milk is produced in those big udders which hang down from the underside of the cow. This milk is the natural food of the baby calf. Fortunately for us the calf does not need all the milk which its mother produces, and after a time it is able to feed on other things instead. The milk from the cow which the calf does not need is taken away from the udders, either by hand milking, or by an electric milking machine. The cow produces the milk in considerable quantity, and if she is not milked regularly, morning and evening, her udders will become so full of milk that the cow will actually be in pain. Farmers who keep cows must milk them twice a day, including holidays and Sundays. After several months the cow will stop giving milk and no new supply will come along until she has had another calf. Then the supply will start all over again.

If the cow did not have this extra milk which the calf does not need we should have no milk puddings, milk chocolate, or bottles of milk at morning break. We are also indebted to the cow for our cream, butter and cheese. Milk is a very good food, and ideal for small babies.

But the new born baby does not have to rely upon the milkman to bring him his milk supply.

A mother provides milk for her babies in just the same way as a cow does for its young. While the baby is growing inside the mother, his mother's breasts are also growing larger. The milk is not ready until the baby is born. But as soon as the baby is ready for some food, his mouth is placed against the nipple of his mother's breasts, and without being taught to do so, he immediately starts to suck. It is instinctive in a new born baby to want to suck anything which is put into his mouth. He sucks his own thumbs or the thumbs or fingers of anyone else if he can get hold of them.

The baby will go on sucking until he has had his fill and then he will stop sucking and allow the nipple to fall from his mouth. Mothers can provide this perfect food for their babies, even in countries where many of the people are very poor and the mother herself is getting barely enough to eat. The baby always likes this sort of food best, knows how to drink it, and knows, too, when he has had enough.

Some babies are fed on special foods, because their mothers are not able to provide enough milk for them, or perhaps they want to go to work and leave the baby in someone else's care. There are several of these patent baby foods on sale in the shops, and some of them are very like the mother's own milk, but it is really less trouble for a mother to feed her baby herself, if she can, and a pleasant experience for her. Whatever kind of milk he is fed with, the baby is held firmly and warmly. He feels that he is loved and that the world is a friendly place.

When Peter and Pamela were born, they were both quite helpless. They could not sit up, or stand, neither could they crawl about. The bones in their bodies were still quite soft and gristly. For a long time they could only lie in their cots or prams, sleeping, kicking, crying, or crowing with pleasure. They needed the loving care of their mothers for a much longer period than most baby animals do.

Lambs, calves and foals can walk very soon after they are born. They are often wobbly at first but within a few minutes they are able to walk quite happily after their mothers. Most four-footed animals are like this. Baby chicks and ducklings are pretty little balls of fluff which can run and peck almost straight away. They have to learn what are the best things to peck, but they are nothing like as dependent upon their mothers as Peter and Pamela and you were.

Some birds are born naked and helpless. You may have seen young nestlings clamouring for food, and the mother and father birds busy going backwards and forwards to the nests with tasty titbits for the youngsters.

Kittens and rats are born blind, and are quite helpless for the first few days of their lives.

The extent to which baby animals are dependent upon their parents varies enormously. But a human baby is dependent on its parents for far longer than any animal.

Peter and Pamela were both fed by their mothers for the first few months of their lives. During that time their first teeth began to come through. These gave Peter a good deal of trouble and he was often fretful at night. Pamela seemed to cut her teeth without much pain. As they grew older they were weaned from feeding at their mothers' breasts. This was necessary, as a baby comes to need a more varied diet if it is to grow strong and vigorous. Their mothers gradually reduced the amount of milk and gave them instead sieved vegetables, fruit, and fine cereals, and rusks to try their teeth on. As their demand for milk decreased, so did the supply, until it finally dried up. From that time onwards their diet was almost like yours.

As the months passed Peter and Pamela grew bigger and stronger. They were soon crawling around the floor, and trying to pull themselves up on their legs, which were still wobbly. This was a great period of exploration. Peter was enormously pleased when he found the coal bucket, and discovered that the black colour came off on his hands. He even tried eating some, and his mother was terribly worried that he might have eaten enough to make himself ill before she found what he was up to.

Pamela distinguished herself by trying to pull herself upright by means of the tablecloth, with the result that she pulled all the teacups and saucers down onto her head. Peter and Pamela's parents had to learn to keep such dangerous things as hanging tablecloths and pan handles, and valuable fragile things out of their babies' reach.

About the same time the babies began to experiment with sounds. Peter achieved a sound which his father was quite certain was 'Dadda' and Pamela repeated 'Mum Mum' with monotonous regularity. After they had learnt to walk and talk, they would often play together quite happily with their toys.

When they were five years old, Peter and Pamela went to school together. Their mothers took them on the first day. Both children felt rather frightened about entering this big and strange new world of the school, where the playground always seemed to be filled with hundreds of other and bigger children all charging about in different directions and yelling loudly about their own affairs.

For the first few days Peter was inclined to be tearful when he left his mother at the school gate, but Pamela liked her school from the first day and was happy to have so many children of her own age to play with and to find such a lot of interesting things to do. Peter settled down after the first week or two and began to enjoy himself. The children gradually learnt to become sensible and unselfish members of the class, and soon came to realize that they must take their turn with the other children and not expect to have the whole of the teacher's attention all the time as they had had their mothers' at home.

Peter and Pamela were happy at school. Soon they were learning to read, to do little sums, to cut out, draw, paint and make models, and they heard many interesting stories of children in other lands, people who had lived a long time ago, and of the wonderful world of nature. The boys and girls played happily together at this age. Peter and Pamela always walked home together, hand in hand, and usually spent the time after school playing in each other's garden or house. They did not give any thought to the fact that one of them was a boy and the other a girl. They were friends, and although Pamela liked playing with her dolls and Peter with his train, they often played with these things together and enjoyed lots of other games besides.

They went up the school together, and were very proud and felt quite grown up when they left the Infant classes and went into the Junior School at the age of seven. By this time they could both read fairly well, although Pamela was somewhat better at this than Peter. He liked sums best, and often got more right than Pamela.

About the age of nine Peter became very interested in football and cricket. He tried to get Pamela to play these games in the garden, but although she would sometimes play with him she did not enjoy the games much, especially football which she thought rather a rough game, and even though Peter tried hard to teach her she never seemed able to kick the ball more than a few feet. Eventually Peter gave it up in disgust, and then instead of walking home with Pamela as he had always done before, he stayed to play football or cricket on the school field after school, and sometimes went with the other boys to play in the recreation ground in the evenings or on Saturdays.

Pamela became a keen Brownie at this time. She also spent a lot of her time skipping or playing other games with her girl friends.

From this time onward they saw far less of each other than they had done before. They still played indoor games together, and shared an interest in collecting stamps, but both of them preferred to play with children of their own sex.

This was a sign that they were both growing up. Up till that time there had been very little difference between them in their physical or mental attainments. They could run at about the same speed. Peter could jump a little further along the playground, and Pamela could jump a little higher.

The fact that one was a boy and the other a girl had not bothered them at all. Soon, however, very important changes were to begin to take place in their bodies. The next chapter deals with the changes in Pamela and the following one with those which Peter will undergo, but both boys and girls should read both chapters as they ought to know what happens to those of the opposite sex as well as their own.

# CHAPTER THREE

## *Pamela Becomes a Young Lady*

By the time Pamela reached her last year at Primary School, she was several inches taller than Peter. This rather worried Peter, who had previously been about the same height as Pamela, and he began to think that he was going to be small. What happened was quite normal. Girls start to turn into young women about two years earlier than boys start to turn into young men.

Most girls suddenly make a big spurt in their growing rate at about the age of eleven. During this period they often grow several inches in height, and in two years may put on as much as two stones in weight. The boys make their spurt about two years later, by which time most girls are reaching the end of their period of rapid growth. Although they do not usually start their spurt until the ages of twelve to fourteen, the boys usually overtake the girls

in both weight and height—very much like a
runner passing those in front of him on the final
straight of a mile race—and when they have
finished growing they are usually bigger than
the girls who, at eleven, were taller and
heavier.

These spurts of growth are brought about by
the action of small glands inside the body
which manufacture liquids called hormones.
One gland in particular, the pituitary gland,
is responsible for the hormones which change
boys and girls into young men and women.

When Pamela was eleven she was, as I said,
taller than Peter. She was also rather heavier.
Other changes, too, were beginning to take
place in her body, and the first really noticeable one was that her breasts began to develop.
As a baby she had small nipples on her chest
just like Peter, but when she was about eleven
she noticed that the upper part of her chest was
beginning to fill out gradually, and by the
time she was thirteen she was wearing a
brassière to keep her breasts firm and give
them a pleasing shape.

Soon her hips began to get bigger, and hair
began to grow underneath her arms and on the

lower part of her abdomen just above the entrance to the vagina. This hair is known as pubic hair, because it grows above a small bone there called the pubic bone, and the period when all these changes are taking place is called puberty.

About this time too Pamela noticed that she seemed to be getting rather plump and that her tummy stuck out more than it used to. She need not have worried because, once again, this was quite normal and usual, and as soon as her hips had widened out her tummy returned to its normal shape.

None of these changes caused Pamela any actual physical discomfort, but one day a small amount of blood passed out of her vagina. Pamela was not surprised by this, because her mother had wisely prepared her to expect it, and had explained why it happened. Pamela knew exactly what to do, and she rightly took it as a sign that all was well with her and that one day she too could become a mother with children of her own.

If you understand a little of the complicated changes that had taken place in Pamela's body, you will be as prepared as she was, and if you are a boy, you will see why girls sometimes need to have a little special consideration after the age of puberty.

In Chapter One we saw that inside a girl's body there are two ovaries, and that these ovaries release one egg each month. The egg is guided along the Fallopian tube towards the womb. About ten days before this happens, the womb has been getting ready for the egg. The lining of the womb has grown considerably, and filled up with blood, ready to provide food for the egg when it arrives.

But the egg will not turn into a baby unless it has been fertilized. You will want to know how this happens, and I will tell you about it in a later chapter; at the moment we are more concerned with what happens to the unfertilized egg and the extra blood supply which has been specially provided to feed it.

The egg waits for a short time in the womb, and then passes out of the body through the vagina. It is too small to be noticed. Before the lining of the womb can be renewed, the old one is scrapped, along with the extra blood supply which is no longer needed, and together they pass out of the body through the vagina. This happens every month, unless the egg is fertilized, and because it occurs monthly it is called menstruation, from the Latin word *mensis*, meaning a month.

Just at first it is likely to be very irregular, and several months may pass after the first flow, before there is another one. But soon it will settle down to a regular occurrence. On the average it happens every twenty-eight days but it may vary considerably, and come more often than this, or even vary from month to month. The flow of blood usually lasts from three to five days, and once it has settled down to a fairly regular time-table it is a good idea for a girl to keep a note of the date so that she will know when to expect her next 'period', as many people call it.

If she knows when her next period is due, she won't be caught unprepared. The menstrual flow is absorbed by a soft pad of gauze and cotton wool, called a sanitary towel. The pad is kept in place by fastening it to a thin elastic belt worn round the waist. Sanitary towels are on sale at chemists' and drapers' shops. They should be changed several times a day, particularly at the beginning of the 'period' when the flow of blood is greatest.

Cleanliness is of great importance as the menstrual flow can give off a noticeable smell when exposed to the air, and during her periods a girl should bath frequently in warm water. There are many old-fashioned beliefs about what a girl should or should not do during her periods of menstruation. One is that she should on no account have a bath or wash her hair, in case her health is disastrously affected. There is no truth in the belief. At this time of the month a girl needs baths more than at others if she hopes to keep clean and fresh, because apart from the menstrual flow, the perspiration or sweat glands seem to increase their activity, and these can also cause offensive odours. She should take special care, however, to avoid catching a chill.

Menstruation is a natural part of every girl's life, and she should continue her normal activities as far as possible. Some girls have no pain or discomfort at all; others have some cramp-like pains and aches, particularly on the first day. Severe pains are not normal, and the girl who has them should consult her doctor, who may be able to help her. But usually she will be able to do all the things she usually does, although she should not exert herself too violently at this time.

It is possible for some girls to swim comfortably during their menstrual periods, but the water should certainly not be too cold, and for many girls it is preferable not to swim at all whilst the flow is at its greatest. In any case, out of consideration for others, it is best not to swim in a swimming bath.

A few girls find it necessary to take things easily for the first day or so, and ask to be excused from strenuous games or physical exercises, because these tire them too much. But girls should try not to make too much of these periods. It is very easy to magnify small aches and pains and imagine that you are less well than you really are. If you keep yourself fit and healthy, the probability is that you will experience very little inconvenience at all.

Girls often feel embarrassed at the time of their menstrual flow, because they are afraid that their boy friends may ask them to go swimming or indulge in some other violent exercise. Boys who do not know about menstruation are often lacking in understanding, as to why Jane, who is very fond of swimming, suddenly says that she can't or won't accompany them to the swimming baths. That is why it is important for a boy to read this chapter—so that he will then more readily understand, and will not press her unduly to accompany him, and cause her unnecessary embarrassment by having to continue to refuse his invitations.

Menstruation does not last throughout a woman's life. She continues to produce eggs until she is between forty and fifty years of age. Then the egg supply gradually stops, and the womb no longer prepares the extra blood supply every month, and as you have probably guessed, the menstrual flow ceases too.

A woman can bear a child from her early teens until middle age, but not normally after that. While she is young, she is strong and vigorous and usually has more patience with a baby. As she gets older she may not want to be worried by the care of a young child, and if the baby were born to her very late in life, she herself might not live long enough to care for it until it is able to look after itself.

When these changes are taking place in a

girl's body she is maturing, that is, she is coming to her full adult state. Her voice may also change at this time and become rather deeper and fuller in tone. She seems at the same time to become rather more responsible and sensible. Pamela certainly did! She was such a sensible and reliable member of the top class at her Primary School that she was made a prefect. She was a very good one too, and carried out all her duties conscientiously and well.

Peter was rather envious when she was made a prefect. He did not achieve this honour, for though he was a likeable lad, he was, at the age of eleven, a real boy and ripe for all sorts of mischief, and his headmaster did not think that he was reliable enough, or that he would set a good enough example to be made a prefect. He was a fine footballer and gained his school colours, but at the age of eleven he remained a boy, whilst Pamela was already becoming a young lady.

# CHAPTER FOUR

# Peter Becomes a Young Man

When Peter was thirteen he suddenly began to grow rapidly. Some of the boys in his class had started to change into young men a year or so earlier, some did not change noticeably until rather later. During the three years from thirteen until sixteen Peter grew seven inches in height and put on just over three stones in weight. By the time that he was sixteen he was taller than many men and he was three inches taller than Pamela.

His body had changed too. His shoulders were wider, and he was proud of the muscles which showed on his arms and legs when he went swimming. These changes were obvious to all, but there were other, equally important changes taking place inside his body, turning him from a boy into a young man.

You will remember that in the last chapter we described the gradual development of the breasts. Peter, and all other males, have small nipples on the chest. These do not develop. They are really only a relic of the earliest days when Peter was still growing inside his mother. At that early stage of development the baby has the beginnings of the organs of both sexes. If it is to become a boy the special male parts develop, but the female ones do not, and the opposite applies if the baby is to become a girl.

A boy does not have the two ovaries which are to be found in girls. He will never produce any eggs, nor will he have the monthly menstrual flow. Instead of ovaries he has two testes, or testicles. These are the male sex glands, and they bring about other masculine characteristics which we will talk about later on. But instead of producing eggs as the ovaries do, the testicles produce sperms.

The testicles are roundish in shape and about the size of a damson or small plum. They are unlike the ovaries, in that instead of being contained inside the body, they are outside it, and hang between the legs in a small bag of skin, called a scrotum.

You can see the testicles quite clearly on many animals, but not on all domestic animals, because sometimes they are removed when the animal is still young to make it more docile, and to make it grow fatter. A farmer does not usually keep many bulls on his farm. They are apt to be very fierce, and do not need much encouragement to charge at you. When a bull calf has had its testicles removed it is called a bullock. The operation, called castration, is quite a painless one. The bullock will grow big and fat and is reared as a meat animal, but it will be no fiercer than a cow.

People who have male cats or toms sometimes have then castrated when they are young. A 'doctored' cat makes a faithful pet, and does not wander far from its home. It is very gentle, and will not snarl at you as a tom-cat sometimes will. A stallion, or male horse, is also apt to be wild and unmanageable, and often horses are castrated too—they are then called geldings. Most male horses on farms and in riding stables are geldings.

Of course castrating an animal may make it more useful and more easily controlled, but a castrated animal has lost its masculinity, and can never breed.

All male animals are born with testicles, but

only the warmer blooded animals keep the testicles outside the body in the pouch-like scrotum. The reason for this is that the main purpose of the testicles is to produce sperms, and the temperature inside the body of a warm blooded animal is too high for the efficient manufacture of the sperms. In the cold blooded animals, such as frogs and reptiles, and in birds, the testicles are right inside the body, in the same way that the ovaries are inside the female body.

This makes it difficult to tell the sex of some animals. Budgerigars are favourite pets these days, and however hard you look, you will see very little difference in their bodies. You can tell which is a male and which is a female by looking at their heads, because above the beak is a little patch of colour near the nostrils known as the cere. In a male budgerigar this is coloured blue, and in a female it is brown. Similarly it is very difficult to tell the male pigeon from the female, but a pigeon fancier will take one look at the shape of the head and tell you instantly which is which. If you have seen hens and cocks together in a chicken run, you will know that the cock is easily distinguish-

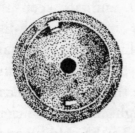

*Diagram* 4

Female egg (or ovum) and Male sperm, both very
highly magnified.

able because the comb on top of its head and
the wattles are more prominent.

Inside the testicles, sperms are made. This
begins when a boy reaches his early teens, and
it goes on all through his life. In this way the
testicles are different from the ovaries which
produce one egg a month over a period of about
thirty years—a total of something like four
hundred eggs. Sperms, on the other hand, are
produced in millions. These sperms are very
tiny and you would need a high-powered
microscope if you wanted to examine them. A
thousand sperms in a straight line would not
cover more than a quarter of an inch. They are
shaped something like tadpoles with tiny heads
and threadlike tails. When they leave the body

they do so in batches of about two hundred million at a time and this amount together would just about fill a tea-spoon.

The sperms leave the male body by means of a tube called the penis. The manufactured sperms are stored in tiny storehouses along the tube which leads from the testicles to the penis, and when they leave the body they are accompanied by a whitish liquid in which they can swim. The whole discharge is known as semen.

The semen passes down a tube which runs through the centre of the penis. This tube also serves another purpose: it is a passageway to the outside of the body for the waste fluids which we call urine, but it is not possible for urine and semen to leave the penis together, as the opening to the bladder in which the waste fluids are stored is closed when semen is discharged.

Normally the penis which hangs down in front of the testicles is limp and soft, but before semen is emitted it becomes much enlarged and stiff. You will find more about this in the next chapter which will tell you how the sperm fertilizes the egg.

The penis of a dog or a bull or a stallion can

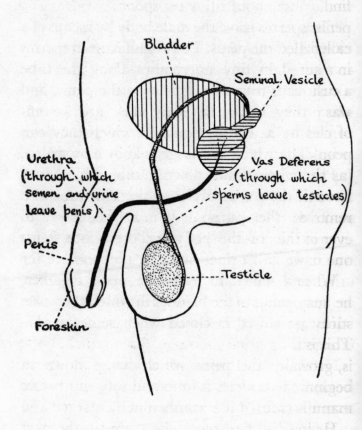

Labels on diagram:
- Bladder
- Seminal Vesicle
- Urethra (through which semen and urine leave penis)
- Vas Deferens (through which sperms leave testicles)
- Penis
- Testicle
- Foreskin

*Diagram 5*
Simplified diagram of the male reproductive organs.

be seen easily. A cat has a penis, too, but it is so small and so well tucked away that it is hard to find. When a baby boy is born the end of his penis is partly covered by a loose skin, which is called the foreskin. This is sometimes cut away in a simple operation shortly after birth. This is a custom which dates back to ancient times, and was probably done in the first place for the sake of cleanliness. It is the custom still with some people that all boy babies should be circumcised (as the operation is called); and all true Jews have this operation. Whether your foreskin was removed or not will make no difference whatever to the possibility of your becoming a father one day.

When a boy reaches the age of about fourteen, he may wake up one morning to find a wet sticky patch on his pyjamas or on the sheet. This is a sign that he is reaching maturity, that is, growing up. It means that his sex glands are beginning to work and that sperms are being manufactured in the testicles.

He may be conscious that he has had a rather strange and exciting dream usually about a girl or a woman. This dream has excited him and caused the penis to ejaculate the sperms. Boys commonly call this a 'wet dream'. These experiences are quite normal and the growing boy should not worry about them.

The millions of sperms which are manufactured will cause him no trouble. Sometimes they leave the body in the form of wet dreams but if the boy is healthy and takes part in games and other forms of vigorous exercise the sperms will be re-absorbed into the body and the wet dreams will not be very frequent.

When Peter was eleven he was a freckle-faced, tousled-haired young rascal. He paid little attention to his appearance, and had to be instructed every morning to run a comb through his unruly hair. His tie, when he wore one, always seemed to be an inch or two below his collar, and he seemed to be totally unaware of the dirt and grime which accumulated daily on his knees and hands.

In spite of all this he had an excellent voice, and was a member of the school choir and also the choir in his local church. On Sunday mornings and evenings, with freshly scrubbed face, and hair persuaded into some semblance of a parting by the use of some of Dad's hair cream, he looked and sounded far more angelic than he really was, and his sweet treble voice soared away above the deeper tones of the older members of the church choir. Although he would never admit it, Peter was secretly very proud of his voice. One day when he was thirteen, he found that it tended to crack on the high notes, and even in talking he was never quite sure what sort of voice would come out when he opened his mouth.

I expect you have guessed that his voice was breaking. No longer would his singing be able to soar above all the rest. Peter's mother was rather sad when his voice began to change and Peter himself was often embarrassed at his sudden squeakiness or gruffness. But he knew that this change was inevitable and that after a few months his voice would settle down again, but would be deeper in tone than formerly. When this happened he would no longer sing the treble parts in the choir, but the bass, baritone or tenor.

This change in the voice can come at any age between about eleven and fourteen. At the same time there are other indications of growing up. Between thirteen and sixteen Peter not only put on a lot of weight and grew considerably in height, but his body began to take on the shape of a man, too, with broadened chest, larger biceps, thigh, and calf muscles. Hair also began to grow underneath his arms, along his forearms and at the base of his abdomen. His legs showed signs of becoming more hairy, and a few stray hairs began to sprout on his chest. Of these he was extremely proud, and rightly regarded them as a sign that he was becoming a man.

But the hairs which interested him most were those which began to appear on his face. At first there was a soft downy growth on his upper lip, and gradually this spread down the sides of his face. He watched these signs of growing masculinity with considerable interest and when he was sixteen, his father suggested that the down was becoming so noticeable on his upper lip that he should have his first shave. So one morning he proudly filled a jug with hot water and proceeded to lather his face, using Dad's shaving brush. Then gingerly he began to scrape away the downy growth with a sharp razor. He found that this was not altogether a pleasant experience, for although the hairs came off quite easily, his lip felt rather sore and naked afterwards, and he cut the top off a small pimple which he had at the corner of his lip.

In spite of this he felt very grown up to have started shaving. The next morning he anxiously inspected his face to see whether the process needed to be repeated. Rather to his disappointment there were no hairs to be seen. He did not have to shave again for nearly a month, but after that the hairs seemed to thicken up and become more bristly, and before he was seventeen he was shaving twice a week. By the time he was eighteen he was shaving every morning, and beginning to resent the time it took. For now that he was shaving regularly he knew that he would have to do so every day for the rest of his life, and although it only took about ten minutes a day, that was over an hour a week, and an hour a week for fifty years or so is quite a sizable chunk out of your life.

Sometimes pimples and spots make shaving difficult. Both boys and girls get pimples more easily in their teens than at any other time. Their number can be greatly reduced by paying attention to what makes a good diet, and if this doesn't help, the doctor should be consulted.

If you could have seen Peter at eleven and again when he was fifteen you would hardly have recognized him. Apart from the physical changes which were taking place, there was also a marked change in Peter's attitude to life in general. He was much more mature and responsible, and he was appointed a prefect at his school, and eventually he was elected House Captain. But the biggest change was in his appearance. He needed no urging now to comb his hair in the mornings. His parting was ruler straight. His tie was neatly knotted, his shoes sparkled, and he spent considerable time and trouble in manicuring his finger nails. He liked smart clothes, and never needed to be reminded to change his shirt when it was dirty. In fact he became rather fussy about his appearance. This increased pride in his appearance was linked with a consciousness that girls, and Pamela in particular, were interesting creatures after all.

I am often asked why it is that men grow hair on their faces and women do not. This is an interesting question, and the only answer that I know goes back to very ancient times. If you look at a stag and a female deer there is no mistaking the male because of his magnificent antlers. A ram can easily be distinguished from a ewe because of its curly horns. These are animals which live in flocks and packs. They are also animals which were often hunted by other, fiercer animals.

Long, long ago when our ancestors lived in caves, they were often attacked by savage animals and other fierce tribes. The cave-man was much hairier than the average male today. If the tribe were scattered, his size and hairiness, together with his deep male voice, were un-mistakable and served as a rallying point for other members of his tribe, in exactly the same way as the stag's antlers and the ram's horns are easily seen by the rest of the flock or herd and serve as a rallying point for them once they are scattered.

Nowadays of course we no longer live in caves, nor do we live in tribes. Our families are unlikely to be scattered among the trees and bushes by a fierce attack, and a father will not have to rally his family around him after they have been scattered. But the grown males still retain these hairy characteristics which have outlived their purpose, and unless he wants to

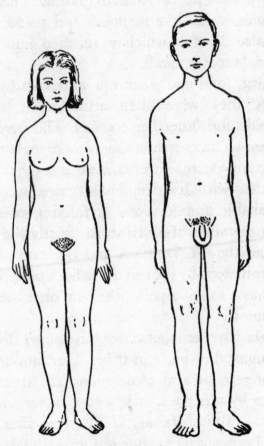

*Diagram 6*
Drawings showing growth and development in girl
and boy of about fifteen.

be hairy like his forefathers, every male must accept the burden of regular shaving.

It is certainly fortunate that hair does not grow on the faces of girls and women. There is occasionally a light down on the upper lip, but this is usually too light to be seen and does nothing to mar the beauty of the female face. But if a woman does not have the irksome necessity of shaving every day, she does have the regular menstrual flow which is, to say the least, inconvenient, and may even cause her some bodily discomfort. Boys therefore should not feel that nature has dealt with them too unkindly when the first thrills of shaving wear off and they settle down to the routine of the daily shave.

You will see from the last two chapters that by the age of about sixteen both Peter and Pamela had changed considerably. They were no longer a boy and a girl, but a young man and a young woman.

# CHAPTER FIVE

# How the Egg is Fertilized

All animal life begins with an egg, but not all eggs will turn into babies. We know that most of the eggs produced by a woman from her early teens until her late forties, numbering some four hundred or so in all, cannot possibly turn into babies. Most of them pass out of her body during her menstrual flow.

Perhaps you had a boiled egg for your breakfast. That egg will never turn into a chick, and it is quite probable that it would never have done so even if you hadn't eaten it. For any egg to hatch into a baby something else is needed.

In the last chapter we saw how a boy in his teens begins to manufacture sperms in his testicles. Before a human baby can be born, the egg from the female must be united with the sperm from the male. When this happens we say that the egg has been fertilized.

Fertilization takes place in many different ways. Perhaps you have seen a stickleback in a pond, or in an aquarium, or even in a tank in the classroom. When it is the breeding season the male stickleback builds a rough nest in the water and persuades the female stickleback to enter the nest and lay her eggs there. Then he enters the nest himself and sprays out his sperms all over the eggs. The sperm cells swim in the water until each reaches an egg which it enters, and in this way fertilization takes place. The sperms and eggs which do not meet very soon die.

A salmon uses a very similar method of fertilization, but in this case the female digs out a little hollow in the bottom of the river-bed where she lays her eggs. The male salmon then plays his part and deposits his sperm on them.

Newts have a very interesting way of ensuring that the sperms reach the eggs to fertilize them. At the mating season the male newt produces its sperms in little transparent envelopes. These packages of sperms he proceeds to hang up on the weed growing in the pond. Having done this he starts to dance in front of the female. He weaves in and out showing his colours, and as the dance goes on the female newt seems to catch some of his excitement. Soon she moves towards the packages of sperms. She picks one up and thrusts it inside her body, where the envelope can burst and the sperms will be free to fertilize the eggs.

Spring is the time when most animals mate. Many of you will have seen frogs' eggs in the classroom at some time or another, particularly if you live in the country. They are like little black specks in the centre of round blobs of jelly. You can find them in spring time in ponds and ditches and if they are kept in a jar you can see them hatch out into young tadpoles, which will in turn change into frogs.

If you are near a pond in spring you might be lucky enough to see how these eggs are fertilized. The eggs are laid by the female in shallow water. When she is ready to lay her eggs, the male frog, which is much smaller, climbs on her back. He grips her tightly with his fingers and thumbs under her arm-pits, and the mass of eggs, or spawn, comes out at the back end of the female. As this happens the male frog sends out a cloud of whitish liquid all over them. This liquid contains the sperms. The sperms swim up to the eggs and burrow down through the jelly to the round black blobs. When a single sperm breaks its way into an egg, it has been fertilized.

In all the ways of mating which we have considered so far the male sperm is able to reach the female egg because it is deposited in water, and can use its long threadlike tail to swim. But this cannot happen with land animals. If the sperm were squirted into the air it would fall to the ground and rapidly die as it dried out. It would never have the chance to fertilize the egg for which it was intended. But the openings into all female bodies are moist enough for the sperm to swim providing it is deposited near enough to do so.

Of course all eggs aren't like frogs' eggs, soft and surrounded by jelly. When a bird's egg is laid, its shell rapidly hardens, but before it grows to its full size in the body of the bird it is small and quite soft—something like a fish's egg. The fertilization of all hard-shell eggs takes place before the shells have formed, and of course this happens while the egg is still in the body of the hen bird.

Perhaps you have seen a cock and a hen mating. You may have thought that they were fighting, or that the cock was in some way punishing the hen. The cock mounts on her back and appears to peck at her head to maintain his balance. This process is rather noisy and involves a good deal of squawking. The cock has no penis, but a small opening under his tail which is really the outer end of his sperm tube. The hen has a similar opening underneath her tail and this is the end of her egg tube. The cock places his opening as near as he can to the opening of the hen and then squirts out his sperm on the feathers around the opening of the hen's egg tube. The sperms are then left to make their way by wriggling and swimming up the hen's egg tube and to fertilize the eggs before the hard shell begins to grow round them.

All birds mate in a similar manner. You may have seen a male and female budgerigar mating. This always seems a most precarious business since they balance on the perch whilst the mating takes place, and if the female hasn't got a firm grip on the perch they sometimes fall off and have to start all over again.

The methods of mating that we have talked about so far rely for their success on the sperms being able to find an egg which is outside the body, as with the fish, or to swim from the outside to the inside of the body, as with the birds. Other animals have a much more efficient method of ensuring that the sperms reach the eggs. This method involves the placing of the sperm tube inside the body of the female before the sperms are released.

The penis is the male sperm tube. Usually it is quite soft and tucked well away for protection on the under side of the animal. But it is filled with lots of tiny spaces and when it is required for the act of mating these spaces fill up with blood, causing the penis to become stiff and much enlarged.

Those of you who live in the country may have seen animals in the act of mating. It is not an uncommon sight to see a dog mounted on the back of a bitch, and if you have seen this happen you may have noticed that the dog's penis is very much larger and stiffer than it is normally. The reason for this is that if the penis were limp it would not be able to enter the vagina, and if it were stiff and rigid all the time it would get in the way and might easily become damaged. So you see that animals are provided with a special but simple way of ensuring that, when fertilization takes place, the sperms have the greatest possible chance of reaching the egg inside the female body.

When a husband and wife love each other it is natural that they should find pleasure in kissing and embracing one another. Instinctively they wish to come together in the closest possible contact. Love making between them sends the extra supply of blood to the husband's penis and also moistens the path to the wife's womb. The penis is then placed inside the vagina (which you will remember is the passage leading up to the womb). It is moved backwards and forwards and rubs against the inside of the vagina. This sends a signal to the testicles to release the sperm, and the act of mating is completed when the sperm is squirted out into the vagina. The sperm then makes its way upwards through the womb and meets the egg in the Fallopian tube. A great number of sperms make this journey at the same time, all seeking the egg to fertilize, but most of the sperms will be wasted as only one can actually enter the egg. The sperms which do not meet an egg linger in the womb or passages leading to it for a day or so, and then die. This act of union in human beings is commonly referred to as sexual intercourse.

# CHAPTER SIX

## *Mating Time*

No one knows what tells an animal when it is time to mate. We say that it is the mating instinct. This is the name we give to strong and little understood forces which cause animals to act in various regular ways.

There are all sorts of instincts and they are born in us as well as in animals. Most of the things we know we have had to learn, either at school or from our parents, or by trial and error. But some things we do not have to learn. A baby does not have to be taught to suck. We say that sucking is instinctive because a baby can do it without any kind of training. Perhaps you do not think that to be able to suck is very clever, but there are many more wonderful examples of instinctive behaviour.

Many birds visit our island only during the summer; they live largely on insects which are plentiful during the warmer months, and when the weather turns colder and there are no more insects flying about for them to catch, the birds fly away to warmer lands. We call these birds which migrate, or fly away for a part of the year, migrants. They seem to sense when they must fly southwards and also when it will be safe for them to return north again. But the most wonderful thing about migration is that when the time for it comes, the parent birds do not escort the younger ones born that summer, as you would expect them to do, to show them the way. The young ones fly off first on their own, and they find their way to Africa across thousands of unknown miles, over strange countries and great seas.

You or I would need lots of maps and would probably ask advice from all sorts of people before we could undertake such a long journey and arrive at the correct destination. Whatever it is which is born in the bird, and which makes it possible for it to accomplish such a difficult task, we call *instinct*.

If a young bird is kept all on its own, and never sees a nest such as similar birds make, that bird will nevertheless build a nest identical to others of the same species, using the same sort of materials in the same sort of way. This is another example of instinctive behaviour. Most animal behaviour is of this kind. They do not have to be shown how to act, and they have no choice about it. Their instincts provide their only pattern of behaviour.

With animals it is instinctive to mate, and the instinct is very often associated with certain seasons of the year, when the sex glands in their bodies become more active. Exactly what causes this activity is still a mystery; but very often it springs up at what seems exactly the right time of year.

Our swifts and swallows return to us in the spring and straight away they begin to mate and set about building nests in readiness for the hen birds to lay their eggs. The spring is by far the best time for the eggs to be laid as the warmer weather lies ahead. The young birds, who are born without any feathers, would not have much chance of surviving if they were hatched out in the middle of winter. Also, insects breed abundantly in the spring so that there is plenty of food for the very hungry youngsters.

Lambs are usually born in the spring, and as it takes about five months from the time of mating for the lamb to be ready to come out into the world, it follows that sheep usually mate in the autumn.

At the mating season, animals attract one another in a variety of interesting ways. If you have a female dog, or as she should be correctly called, a bitch, you may have noticed that she is more sought after by male dogs at certain times of the year. The reason for this is that when the eggs are ready to be fertilized, the bitch gives off a particular smell which attracts the attention of males. When she is in this condition we say that she is 'on heat'. These periods, when the eggs are ready for fertilization, occur about twice a year.

At these times it is very important that you should take good care of the bitch, and if you want pure-bred puppies she must be kept away from male dogs of a different breed, or you will find yourself with a litter of mongrels or of cross breeds. You have probably noticed that when dogs pass each other in the street they will often sniff at one another. They do this to find out if the female is ready for the act of mating.

Animals may attract each other by an appeal

to one of the senses: hearing, feeling, seeing or smelling. The attraction of the bitch for the male dog is an obvious example of an appeal to the sense of smell.

If you have heard a male frog croaking, you will probably have thought that the sound was not very attractive. But it is to a female frog! In spring the male frog croaks away his love song to the female and then they both enter the shallow water and mate as I described to you in the last chapter.

Birds offer a more easily understood example of attraction, by an appeal to the sense of hearing. With most birds the song of the male usually plays a very important part in their courtships. The mating song in spring is very distinctive and bird watchers can readily distinguish the song of one species from another. The spider gives an example of attraction by an appeal to the sense of touch. The male spider will agitate his web to attract the female.

But the commonest method of courtship or attraction is perhaps by an appeal to the sense of sight. Many birds and animals, particularly the males, become much more colourful during the breeding season. The peacock displays his beautiful plumage to the female. The newt exhibits the attractively coloured underside of his body to the female newt. Many male birds become more brightly coloured in spring and even the budgerigars show that they are ready for mating when the ceres above their nostrils turn bright blue, in the case of the males, and a rich brown in the case of the females.

The patterns we find among animal families vary enormously. The mother frog has finished with her babies when she has laid her eggs. The spawn may be eaten by other animals, but she won't know or, apparently, care. The tadpole also has many enemies, but no parents are there to protect or feed it. However, so many are produced each year that even though only a limited number become adult frogs this is enough to keep the frog species going. It is only by chance that the same male and female parents will mate again. In some cases even when animals are born alive, as with the offspring of a guppy—a tropical fish—the mother does not know her own offspring and will readily eat them if they swim unwarily in front of her, and so will the father. Hens will sometimes eat their own eggs which is very much the same sort of thing, and even a bitch will sometimes kill her puppies by sitting on them clumsily.

A dog will mate with a bitch, or a tom-cat with a female cat, but only the mothers will play any part in caring for the young, and then only for a very limited period until the young ones are old enough to fend for themselves.

Roughly speaking, the larger the animal, the longer this period is. The lion will keep its cubs in the pride up to three years, and is usually mated to three or four lionesses for life. But this is unusual. A few birds stay for several seasons with the same mate, but the usual pattern among animals is that the mate is only temporary and the feeling of responsibility for the young, even in the mother, soon dies.

Birds generally make good parents. The father looks after the mother while she is sitting on her eggs, and helps her to feed the greedy youngsters. Among penguins the father takes on most of the job of bringing up the family. Some birds will defend their young as vigorously and as furiously as they are able against anyone or anything which may threaten them. But even with birds the relationship between the parents and the young does not last very long. In a very few months the baby birds are fully fledged and able to fly, and it is not long before they leave their parents, some to fly thousands of miles to the south to winter there. Swans and robins, after rearing their young, will actually turn against them. They regard their own stretch of the river, or their own piece of garden, as exclusively their own, and they will not tolerate any intrusion even from their own offspring once they are old enough to look after themselves.

Although there is great variety in the way animals behave, throughout the whole animal kingdom we find none which care for their young for so long or in so many different ways as humans do. Human parents have a duty to their children to look after them, care for them and provide for them for something like twenty years and that is a very big and a very serious responsibility to undertake. That is one of the reasons why human beings do not choose their mates for short periods only, and before they set up home together they go through a cere- mony of marriage in which each promises to look after the other and remain faithful through- out their life together.

An animal can mate—and normally does so—just as soon as it is physically old enough. It knows instinctively how to prepare for its young and look after them. Human beings are different in this respect. Although it is physically possible for a boy and girl of fifteen to mate and produce a child, they are not ready to care for it at that age. They are not in a position to provide the home, food and clothing that a child needs, nor are they ready to give up their time to caring for a baby—washing, ironing, mending, sewing and cooking; or in the case of a boy, to earning enough money to pay all the household bills.

Most boys and girls of eleven or twelve cannot imagine that they would ever want to spend the rest of their lives living with a person of the opposite sex. At this period in their lives they may well think that the opposite sex are rather silly and futile creatures.

Girls think that boys are rough and noisy. They seem to like boisterous games which most girls do not enjoy. The eleven year old boy is often careless of his appearance, neglects to comb his hair, wash his knees or the back of his neck. He is interested in mechanical things, like aeroplanes, cars, trains and boats. He knows that a girl does not share these interests, and he rather looks down on her lack of knowledge and interest in this direction.

He thinks that girls are rather stupid creatures, inclined to giggle in groups over silly little jokes. He regards as babyish their interest in dolls, clothes, cooking, needlework and knitting. He prefers parties of boys to mixed parties, and is horrified if it is suggested in a game that he should partner a girl or that she should sit on his lap.

Gradually however a change comes about in the feelings of one sex for the other. I described in Chapter Four how, in his early teens, Peter began to comb his hair without being told, and to keep it in place with cream. This he did quite voluntarily for the first time in his life. You remember that he began to show an interest in the colour and types of clothing he wore and spent a considerable period tying his carefully selected tie so that the knot was in the correct place, and not an inch below the collar where he had worn it carelessly for years. He began to ask for brightly coloured sweaters, a duffle coat and a smart pair of shoes.

All these things happened very gradually, but they were another sign to Peter's parents that he was growing up. He still professed a lack of interest in girls, but in spite of this he could often be seen in deep conversation with Pamela, and when he was sixteen her photograph suddenly appeared on his dressing-table.

Pamela also underwent a change, or rather a number of changes at this time. She had always been rather more interested in her appearance than Peter, and in her early teens she used to spend considerable periods brushing her fair wavy hair and arranging it in different styles. She borrowed some of her mother's face powder and even tried a few experiments with lipstick and nail varnish. Her interest in clothes also increased. At fifteen she had her first pair of nylons and worried her mother daily until she received a pair of shoes with high heels. Her wardrobe increased rapidly with a multitude of pretty dresses, skirts, blouses and jumpers. Although she had always considered football a rough game, she now watched the matches in which Peter played, and she even volunteered to help with the teas at the cricket matches in which he took part. She became interested in singers and film stars, and her bedroom always had a picture gallery of her favourite stars.

Both Peter and Pamela in their teens were becoming increasingly conscious of and interested in the opposite sex. Their interest in their appearance and the extra care they took to make themselves attractive were of course somewhat similar to the methods of courtship display of some animals and birds. They were in fact going through the preliminary stages of attracting a mate.

It may seem impossible to you at eleven that in a few years time you may deliberately seek out the companionship of one of the opposite sex, but it will certainly happen to most of you. There will come a time when you feel that you cannot be really happy or enjoy any activity to the full unless you are with one certain boy or girl. In other words you will fall in love.

On television, in films and books you will certainly have read of or seen this happening to other people, and probably thought that it couldn't possibly happen to you. But it does happen to most people. The girls will be attracted by handsome young men and the boys by good-looking young women. But merely to be attracted by the outward appearance of someone is not the same as falling in love, although many people think so. Far too often people who do not really know one another are attracted to each other by outward appearances, a pretty face, a trim figure, wavy hair or a handsome profile. Such people often get married after a surprisingly short courtship only to find out afterwards that in spite of the magnificent looks of their partner, he or she is not a very nice person to live with, and their marriage is an unhappy one.

If we chose our mates merely for the act of of mating, and could choose afresh each year, a mere physical attraction of one for the other would be sufficient; but two people who marry and set up house together have agreed to live together for the rest of their lives. They depend on one another for their happiness, and hope to share all the joy as well as the responsibilities which come from having babies. A person may have good looks, and be amusing, but if this is all it isn't much to contribute to the wonderful experience of marriage and parenthood.

A boy and girl who are attracted to one

another should get to know one another very well indeed before they think about marriage. They should find out what are each other's tastes, habits, likes and dislikes, temper and temperament. Just imagine for a moment that you had to face every morning and evening of your life the prospect of sitting opposite someone who was selfish and bad tempered, or that you had to live with someone whose interests were entirely different from yours. A boy usually chooses a boy friend and a girl a girl friend because they have many interests in common. How much more important it is therefore that in a life partner these things should also be considered very carefully.

You will be thinking that all these things are very far in the future as far as you are concerned. That is true, but it won't be as long as you think before you are attracted to someone of the opposite sex. This will be natural and right. You should have lots of friends so that when you do fall in love and decide to get married, you will have selected the right one to form a lasting partnership with you.

# CHAPTER SEVEN

# *Heredity*

When Peter was eight years old, he was delighted to have a baby brother. After much discussion, it was decided to call him Robin. Peter was rather disappointed the first time he saw Robin in his cot, soon after he had been born. The baby was so tiny, with a little puckered-up red face, and no hair to speak of at all. Peter had generously taken his old Teddy bear to present to the new baby, and was rather hurt that Robin took no interest in his present.

His mother explained to him that when he was a little older Robin would probably be delighted with the bear, and this proved to be true.

A few weeks later Robin was taken for his first walk in his new pram by his mother and father, and Peter proudly accompanied them. They had not gone far before they met some friends who, of course, wanted to see the new baby. After Robin had been duly admired the friends agreed that he was just like his father and the very image of what Peter had been at the same age.

Peter took another look under the hood of the pram. He studied Robin's features very carefully and then looked up at his father. He could see no similarity whatever, and as for looking like him, he felt quite sure that even as a tiny baby he had never looked like Robin.

The walk continued. The next people they met were Pamela and her parents. Again the pram stopped and Robin was carefully inspected. Pamela's mother declared that Robin was just like his mother.

Peter looked at her in astonishment. Grown-ups certainly said the strangest things. He listened to their conversation for a while and then went and sat on a low wall nearby, where Pamela soon joined him.

'I think your baby brother is lovely, don't you, Peter?'

'Oh, he's all right, I suppose,' replied Peter. 'But he doesn't half yell at night. Wakes me up and keeps me awake.'

'I wish I had a baby brother or sister,' said Pamela, wistfully.

'Perhaps you will have one day,' replied Peter. 'Then they'll talk a lot of nonsense about him, too, I expect.'

'What nonsense?'

'Well, didn't you hear your Mum say Robin was just like my Mum? We've just seen Mr. and Mrs. Richards and they said he was like my Dad, and the exact image of me when I was a baby. Well, I ask you? My Mum and Dad aren't the same to look at, are they?'

'No,' replied Pamela. Peter's father was tall and rather thin with a pale face and curly black hair. Peter's mother was much shorter, with a pretty face, blue eyes and a mop of pale golden hair.

'Well then,' went on Peter, 'if they aren't the same how can Robin look like both of them?'

'I don't know.'

'Course not. He can't and he doesn't. I told you they talked a lot of nonsense. They just say these things for something to say.'

There the conversation ended and the walk was resumed. But Peter, for all his clever reasoning, was not right in his deductions.

Robin could and did look something like both of his parents and like Peter too, although when he grew older there were many noticeable differences between them. We know quite a lot about how these similarities occur in families.

You know that animals always produce babies of their own kind. A cat will always produce kittens, never puppies or chicks. A cow will have a calf and never a foal and so on.

But suppose a spaniel dog is mated with a fox terrier. The puppies will of course all be dogs, but do you know what they will look like? Will they be spaniels or fox terriers? Or will they be a mixture of both? The odds are that there will be something of both parents clearly visible in the puppies although some of them will more nearly resemble spaniels, and some fox terriers. Somehow or other both parents will have contributed something to their looks.

You know that unborn babies spend the first few months of their growth inside their mothers' bodies, until they are big and strong enough to come into the outside world. It is perhaps not surprising that they should therefore bear some resemblance to their mothers. But as a matter of fact, so far as we know the resemblances do not arise while the embryo is growing inside the mother's body. They are already contained in the egg. Just as all that the father contributed to their being was contained in a microscopic sperm. Somehow or other the many characteristics which a child inherits from its parents are transmitted by means of the sperm and the egg.

If you could examine a mother's egg cell or a father's sperm cell under a high-powered microscope you would see that each cell contained a number of minute, threadlike objects. These are called chromosomes. There are twenty-three of these in the egg cell and twenty-three in the sperm cell, and when the egg and the sperm unite the fertilized egg cell has forty-six chromosomes.

Each chromosome carries a number of even smaller pieces called genes. These genes determine what the baby shall look like. Each gene carries with it some characteristic passed on from the parent, but no chromosome can carry exactly the same sorts of genes. There are millions and millions of possible combinations which can be handed on and it is not surprising therefore that we are all somewhat different from each other.

Thus you will see that it was quite possible for Robin, Peter's young brother, to inherit some characteristics from both his parents, and whilst his father and mother do not look in the least alike, Robin may bear a distinct resemblance to both of them.

This is complicated and it is made even more so because some of the characteristics carried by the genes are stronger than others. When this is so we say that these are dominant genes and carry dominant characteristics. For example, the gene which carries the brown-eyed characteristic is dominant over one carrying a blue-eyed characteristic. It is therefore likely that if one of the parents has blue eyes and one brown eyes, the children will have brown eyes, but this is not always the case.

The laws which govern inheritance were first discovered by an Austrian monk named Mendel. He experimented over a number of years mainly with easily controlled plants such as peas. In one of his experiments he mated a tall pea with a dwarf pea. The result was not as you might expect—a mixture—but he found that all the peas in the next generation were tall. On mating this generation he found that he obtained three tall peas to one dwarf pea in the second generation. The short peas continued to breed true together and never produced any tall peas. Of the tall peas one-third bred all tall peas and the other two-thirds continued to produce peas in the ratio of three tall to one dwarf. Tallness was therefore dominant over dwarfness. In the first generation, the dwarf characteristic was not lost altogether, but lay dormant, only to reappear in the second generation.

This explains why it is possible for two dark-haired parents to produce a child with fair hair, or why two short parents may have a tall son.

All the characteristics which we receive from our parents do not necessarily show themselves in us, but may show themselves again in our children or grandchildren.

You will see therefore that what we look like, how big we are, whether we have curly hair or straight hair, or a long nose or a short one, is decided long before we are born, at the moment when the egg cell and the sperm cell unite. You must not think however that your parents are responsible for all your faults as well as your looks. What a person becomes depends to some extent on his upbringing and to some extent on himself. If you are by nature bad tempered and surly, it is not impossible to prevent yourself from being so, even though it may require a real effort on your part. If your father is short tempered and your mother unpunctual, there is no reason whatever why you should be either. It all depends on you!

One other thing is also decided at the moment that the egg cell and the sperm cell unite, and that is whether the unborn baby shall be a boy or a girl. This is governed entirely by what sort of sperm cell unites with the egg. About half the sperm cells have a special chromosome called the Y chromosome and these sperm cells will produce boy babies. The other half of the sperm cells have what are called X chromosomes and these will produce girl babies. You will see that it is purely a matter of luck which of the thousands of sperm cells manages to reach the egg first. Whichever type of sperm cell it is will decide the sex of the unborn baby.

Some parents have a preference for either a boy or a girl, but they have absolutely no choice in the matter, and nothing that anyone can do ensures that a baby shall be the sex they wish for. This is perhaps just as well or we might find ourselves with too many girls or too many boys, whereas at the moment there are roughly equal numbers born; approximately 103 boys to every 100 girls.

When you think of the small number of features which go to make up the human face, it seems incredible that we can all still be different from one another, and that nowhere in the world is there another human being exactly like you.

If you have brothers or sisters you probably have some similarity to them which you have been told about or which you can see for yourself, but even your brothers and sisters are not identical with you, unless you happen to be one of a pair of identical twins.

There are two sorts of twins: those who are identical or very nearly so, and who are always of the same sex, and those who are no more alike than any other brothers and sisters and may be of different sexes.

To be identical, two children must share the same chromosomes. They are born from one egg and not two. Very early during its development the egg splits into two separate parts, each possessing exactly the same set of chromosomes, and the children when they are born are so similar that it is often difficult even for their mother to tell them apart. Because they came from the same egg they were fertilized by the same sperm cell—one only—and this sperm cell carried either the X or the Y chromosome, but certainly not both. Hence identical twins must both be boys or both girls.

Sometimes, however, twins are born who are of different sexes and often very different from one another in appearance. When this happens it is because there were by chance two eggs ready for fertilization at the same time. Each of these eggs had its own set of chromosomes and each was fertilized by a different sperm. Each sperm also had its own set of chromosomes, including the X or the Y chromosomes. This sort of twins can therefore be of different sexes and the children will be as different in appearance as any other brothers and sisters.

Identical twins are much rarer than twins of the other kind. The latter occur once in about a hundred births whereas identical twins occur once in two or three hundred births. Some families have twins much more frequently than others. This is because the ability to have them is a characteristic which, like any other, is carried in a gene.

I expect you have read in the paper at one time or another of the birth of triplets, quads and even quins. These are very rare indeed, and they may be formed in either of the two ways applicable to twins; that is, they may be formed by one egg breaking into several parts or from several eggs which were ready for fertilization at the same time.

It is perhaps fortunate that children are not often born as quads or quins, for few mothers would be able, without assistance, to care for four or five young babies at the same time. Even one baby absorbs most of a mother's time and attention. Also the baby stays inside its mother's womb for nine months and is quite large when he comes into the outside world. There is not room inside a mother's body for many children unless they are very much smaller than the normal seven pound baby. When quins or quads are born they are usually much smaller and may weigh only a pound or so. This means that they are not really ready to face the outside world and such tiny babies have to be kept in special incubators in hospitals until they have grown nearer to the normal birth size.

Cats and dogs have litters of several kittens and puppies, but they are all very small when they are born and do not need much care and attention apart from feeding and keeping warm. In a few weeks they are big and strong enough to leave their parents, and when this happens the parents' responsibilities are at an end. This, of course, is not the case with human babies. When many young are produced at the same time, it is likely that only a few of them will survive.

A fish may lay thousands of eggs, but many of these will be eaten before they hatch out and many more will also be eaten when they are very small. The mother is not bothered by her large family for she has no responsibility for their upbringing at all. They must fend for themselves from the start.

You will see that there are several circumstances which decide the number of babies a mother can produce at once. There is the size of the womb and the size of the baby when it is born; there is the amount of care and attention the baby will need and the length of time during which the mother must care for it; and finally there is the chance of survival which the offspring will have after they are born.

\*      \*      \*

You are now on the verge of changing from children into young men and women. I hope this book will have helped you to understand the wonderful story of your birth and the changes which will take place in your bodies and outlooks as you pass into manhood and womanhood. I hope that as you grow older you will make many friends of the opposite sex and that when the time comes for you to choose a mate you will choose wisely and well. You will then have that joy in your marriage and your children which is unequalled by any other sort of happiness.